KURACCA

Running Water Community Press
Central Arrernte Land
9 Hele Crescent
Ciccone Northern Territory 0870
contact@runningwatercommunitypress.com
www.runningwatercommunitypress.com

Published by Running Water Community Press 2023

Edited by Us Mob Writing, Samantha Faulkner and Marissa McDowell as well as Michelle Hyde, HD Writing and Educational Services

Cover artwork and insert: Belinda Nelson-McDowell
Title: 'Yinaagalang-dhu yarra giilang-galang ngurambang-ga'
Artwork description: The artwork is about many Indigenous women gathering together and telling story on Country. These women are from the bush, desert, saltwater and freshwater Country from across the nation.
Wiradjuri translation: Elaine Patricia Lomas and Letetia Harris. *A New Wiradjuri Dictionary* compiled by Dr Stan Grant Snr and Dr John Rudder 2010.

Book design: Gemma Banks, Marissa McDowell
Printed in Australia by McPherson's Printing Pty Ltd
ISBN: 978-0-6480629-7-4

Running Water Community Press is a not-for-profit community-controlled publisher based in Mparntwe/Alice Springs that is run by First Nations storytellers, poets and writers.

This project has been supported by the Aboriginal and Torres Strait Islander Leadership Grant from the Australian Capital Territory Government and Arts Activities Funding from artsACT.

Supported by

US MOB WRITING
FIRST NATION VOICES

KURACCA

Running Water Community Press pays respect to First Nations peoples as the first storytellers and the sovereign owners and custodians of this continent. This book was written on Ngunnawal and Ngambri lands and was published on Central Arrernte land. It was printed on Dja Dja Wurrung land. It will be read across the sovereign lands of many First Nations peoples. We honour Elders past, present and emerging, and express our commitment to ongoing struggles for justice, repatriation, community control and truth-telling.

First Nations readers should note that this work contains the names and images of people who have passed away.

CONTENTS

ACKNOWLEDGEMENT

I would like to acknowledge the Aboriginal people as the traditional custodians of this, their homeland, on which we now live and work.

As we acknowledge Country we are reminded of the importance of Country for Aboriginal people. Country is the tangible gift from the Creator Spirit which supports and sustains us. Country brings Aboriginal people together to sing, dance and paint their stories of thanksgiving to the Creator Spirit for the gift of life and of all living things.

We acknowledge the Ancestors and Elders who were and continue to be the storytellers of this land and its people. They help us to know our Country and people of the past and our present more clearly.

Finally, we are reminded of the journey that began with the Aboriginal people in this land, but that now incorporates the larger family of Australian people.

– Aunty Kerry Reed-Gilbert, from *Biamies Dreaming* © 1997

Vale Aunty Kerry Reed-Gilbert
24 October 1956 – 13 July 2019
Image © Marissa McDowell
Apology Concert Ten Year Anniversary
Canberra 2018

TRIBUTE

This anthology *Kuracca* (the white sulphur crested cockatoo) is dedicated to the late Aunty Kerry Reed-Gilbert, Wiradjuri warrior, writer, poet, author, activist and leader in the writing arena. She has nurtured, inspired and encouraged First Nation writers from across the country. Aunty Kerry leaves behind a lasting legacy of literature and a generation of writers that she has supported.

Kuracca is Aunty Kerry Reed-Gilbert's totem, after which she named her business 'Kuracca Consultancy'. The white sulphur crested cockatoo is a constant reminder of her presence.

Aunty Kerry was a member of Us Mob Writing which was initially established in 1997 as a local Indigenous writers group. Us Mob Writing is one of Canberra's longest running published writing groups that continues to write contemporary prose, poetry and literature.

Us Mob Writing would like to acknowledge Aunty Kerry Reed-Gilbert's tireless effort in supporting Australian First Nation writers.

FOREWORD

When I was first approached by members of Us Mob Writing to read over the complete manuscript for which you are holding in your hands right now — I read it and re-read it across continents of foreign sands adjunct to linoleum shining seas, before glazed mountain-tops I would hold my eyes wide-shut. I would sit still. I would hear my sistas and tiddas reading to me their verses one at a time. I would reflect. Holding within my very grip were the ancient fibres of words — the scent of clever bark, language, ceremonial lines, humour, loss and love, pain and gain woven into a most elongated shared herstory of Australian First Nations' poetry as prescribed by Aboriginal and Torres Strait Islander women. *The Tree of Knowledge* by the late Kerry Reed-Gilbert truly opens the edges of this creation and invites you, the reader, to have a seat if you dare, at the table of these eleven outstanding poets lead by the immeasurable Marissa McDowell, proud niece of Kerry Reed-Gilbert.

The poetry and prose awaiting your creative cultural engagement, all sixty-five poems in content equates to some sixty-five thousand years and beyond of what it means to be here in the now, as Aboriginal and Torres Strait Islander women representing their families, communities, heritage, their shadows, their promise, their matriarch, themselves — it is within these pages you shall find what it means for all of us to be alive and thriving through chapters of millennia as spoken and written by Us Mob Writing.

I acknowledge that upon the wings of the great white sulphur-crested cockatoo Kuracca we meet at the spiritual intersection of Kerry Reed-Gilbert's legacy. Her beloved Kuracca connected Us Mob Writing and First Nations Australia Writers Network in ways no one could have possibly seen nor forecast. Intrinsically our poetry is our first skin — Belinda Nelson-McDowell, twin sister to Marissa has captured this most magisterial storytelling painting of women belonging, of yarning, of gathering so preciously in her cover design artwork titled 'Yinaagalang-dhu yarra giilang-galang ngurambang-ga'.

The Anthology, the Collection, the Book — Editor, Samantha Faulkner meticulously corralled the finest gems from within Us Mob Writing to share with you throughout. As penned by Sam on page 56,

Languages, art, culture, knowledge
Our gifts to the nation
If only you'd listen
Always was, always will be!

And to you the reader, now held within your very own grip are the collective breaths from Us Mob Writing — fibres of inherent words, the ongoing scent of clever bark, the truest of gifts that keeps on giving. Hear their words.

– Yvette Holt, Chairperson, First Nations Australia Writers Network

PREFACE

This book features a collection of poetry and prose written by members of Us Mob Writing group to showcase our unique and diverse style as First Nation writers, poets and storytellers from across Australian lands and seas.

Vale, Aunty Kerry Reed-Gilbert, co-founder of Us Mob Writing, and inaugural Chairperson.

Aunty Kerry Reed-Gilbert dedicated her life to supporting and championing writers from across the nations. During her final days whilst in a hospice, she told me that she had applied for an Aboriginal and Torres Strait Islander Leadership Grant from the Australian Capital Territory Government on my behalf so that I could continue her legacy and bring national awareness to how deadly Us Mob Writing is.

By receiving this opportunity, it has given me the experience to compile and publish my first book which has not only been a learning process but also cathartic at the same time.

Of course, nothing is ever achieved without the ongoing support of community: Us Mob Writing, First Nations Australia Writers Network, and Running Water Community Press and their wonderful graphic and publishing team have greatly assisted in their roles as midwives to the birthing of *Kuracca*. The inspiration for the title of this book *Kuracca*, meaning white sulphur-crested cockatoo, came from Aunty Kerry Reed-Gilbert's totem after which she also named her successful consultancy business. I wanted to attribute the book to her by incorporating her totem and her written work.

The featured Wiradjuri artwork 'Yinaagalang-dhu yarra giilang-galang ngurambang-ga' was commissioned from my twin sister Belinda Nelson McDowell. Having consulted with Aunty Elaine Patricia Lomas and Letitia Harris for Wiradjuri translations for this particular artwork. This artwork strongly compliments the contents. It was important for me to include my family in this process in the same way that I attribute my writing to my three daughters and my poodle cross kelpie named Russell.

The endorsements on the back cover as well as the foreword are written by some of Aunty Kerry's close friends who have known her in the writing arena for many years. Lesa Reed, her daughter, also endorses the book.

My hope is that this book brings as much joy to those reading it as it has given me to compile it and release it.

MMcDowell

– Marissa McDowell, Chairperson, Us Mob Writing

KERRY REED-GILBERT

"There is no instruction manual or self help booklet on what makes a leader."

"The best: just write. The worst: just write – it's not as easy as that."

A Wiradjuri woman from Central New South Wales, Aunty Kerry performed and conducted writing workshops nationally and internationally. She was the co-founder and inaugural Chairperson of First Nations Australia Writers Network 2012–2015. A member of Us Mob Writing, initially established in 1997 as a local Indigenous writers group. In 2013, she co-edited *By Close of Business*, and was co-editor for the *Ora Nui Special Edition: A Collection of Māori and Aboriginal Literature*. In 2015, her short story was listed for the Story Wine Prize. Aunty Kerry edited *A Pocketful of Leadership in the ACT* (2016) and *A Pocketful of Leadership in First Nations Australia Communities* (2017).

Aunty Kerry wrote her biography *The Cherry Picker's Daughter* in 2019. She was a member of the Aboriginal Studies Press Advisory Committee and her poetry and prose have been published in many journals and anthologies nationally and internationally, including in the *Macquarie PEN Anthology of Australian Literature*.

Her works have been translated in French, Korean, Bengali, Dutch and other languages.

Image © Marissa McDowell. Quote 1 from: *A Pocketful of Leadership in First Nations Australia Communities.* Edited by Kerry Reed-Gilbert 2017. Quote 2 from: The Wheeler Centre – www.wheelercentre.com (Interview) *Working with Words:* Kerry Reed-Gilbert 2015

THE TREE OF KNOWLEDGE

Look here that my story
my story been here for thousands of years
story right there in front of you
that tree full of knowledge telling you story about country
story about creation
story about belonging
but you blind you not see
your eyes blinked because there's no book, no pages
you don't see it cause it aint bound with white man's string

WRAP ME IN THE UNIVERSE

I am but a spec in the universe of life
I tremble as each day awakens
I grow stronger with each new dawn
life nurtures my existence
I seek my place in the landscape of living
I am withered ageless as time beginning
I wrap you into my skin as you foster life within my limbs
I reached to touch the world as the sun's rays kiss the earth
my love embraces you this sun bleached country
my home of the dreaming
I am kissed by the sun gentleness surrounds my being
peaceful winds bring the eve of the night as I lay my spirit
down to rest
stars shimmer like diamonds
life's joys encased with each memory
I give thanks to mother earth

WIRADJURI COUNTRY

1,000ks Wiradjuri country
eagles, angels, sun bursts,
gum trees, geraniums
and a pocket full of poetry.
I travel my country,
my land,
my life,
my religion.

The bush calls me back
to the time of before.
before tar and cement.
brick walls and tin roofs.
to the time of Creation
where men were men
and honesty was Lore.

Wiradjuri country,
Spirit of the earth.
Red dirt, dignity.
Truth and justice.
Lores of the land.

The wind whispers
as it captures me
reaching deep into my soul

thousands of years
of memories enter my spirit
as they guide me through country.

Dignity and pride as I stand proud
before my Elders of long time past
I honour them with dignity and courage
as I walk upon my land.
I am Wiradjuri.

Previously published in *States of Poetry – Series Two 2017 – Australian Capital Territory*

LISA FULLER

"Just write. Two simple words, yet they feel so impossible. Find help with fellow writers, books, workshops, podcasts, etc. Make the time, figure out what works for you. You can do it."

Lisa is a Wuilli Wuilli woman from Eidsvold, Queensland, also descended from Wakka Wakka and Gooreng Gooreng peoples. She's lived on Ngunnawal and Ngambri lands (Canberra) since 2006 and is undertaking her PhD in Creative Writing at the University of Canberra. Lisa has won a number of awards, including the 2017 David Unaipon Award for an unpublished Indigenous writer.

Her debut novel, *Ghost Bird*, won several awards, including the 2020 Australian Capital Territory Book of the Year and the 2020 Queensland Literary Awards. It was also an Honour Book in the 2020 Children's Book Council of Australia in the Book of the Year Older Readers category and was shortlisted for a number of other awards. *Ghost Bird* was released in the United Kingdom in October 2021.

Lisa wears many hats in pursuit of her writing, including sessional academic, freelance writer, editor and consultant. She has essays, short stories and poetry published across a number of publications. She has been a member of Us Mob Writing since 2011.

NOT YET

A still place
inside the snake pit
of my gut
never felt
never known
muscles move that
ways before
couldn't understand
my body
not mine
and how?
sprinkles then floods
washing hope out
in sunset colours
strange and textured
didn't know
no one told
it could be like this.

GORN THEN

Push out
Fuck off
Cut from your life
like a cancerous
mass of unwanted
soiled tissues
and for what?

Erase me
blame me
tell me I'm wrong
gouge thick nails
into skin and wrench
outwards rip them
from me like chunks
of fleshy darkness
spew vitriol on me
Again.

Each time you do
it hurts less
and less.
Want it not to matter
Should always matter
on the brink
When will it end?

LIQUID GOLD

Soothing stress-relieving
pouring warmth
hits empty stomach
no time no time
to talk
to eat
to breathe
Just drink.
Swallow the surface
feelings into guts
twisted and coiled
not grog or smokes
no pokies or drugs
safer. Apparently.
Rush to each crisis
another another
don't think or feel
Just drink.

DINING OUT

Fresh foods and drinks dance
On tongues wagging, sharing laughs
Life, love. Connecting

LUNA

In the depths of misery
a small figure
wriggling bum and tail
a warm nose
pushed into faces
swift licks and run away
fingernails scratch
scratch
the furry little body
soft burring speech and snores
talking clearly of hunger
excitement, energy
clownish gambolling
joy personified
twenty kilos of love
our little foster fail

NUMB

A screen
Any one will do
It's glowing feckless
Horror
Pixel addict
it calls
You answer
lose yourself
your thoughts
your pain
sit waiting for
your eyes to
look away.
So you don't.
You sit there
right in front of me
But you're gone.

ACKNOWLEDGEMENT OF THEIR COUNTRY

Walk the meeting place
Ngunnawal and Ngambri land
Care for Country, all

HOPE

Danger all
beware and heed
the worst word
in their dictionary
tears your flesh
damage the soul
an aching loss
helpless
Unknown/unwhole

That word will tempt
glisten and shimmer
entice you to follow
head you into danger
Don't go!

Stay safe in your pain
stay put in your place
where they made you
get comfortable
Play only their game
stick with the known
Be grateful
Be silent
Known pain
won't hurt the
way Hope can.

WITH YOU

You enfold me
those arms, that chest
No clichés, your embrace
your smell, your heat
Heartbeat bumps my ear
brushing fingers
soft lips to my hair
my forehead
my nose
my cheek
Hands laced with mine
rougher, larger
whispers
Are you okay?
under voice
how can I help?
please talk to me
You search me out
find my hiding place
no demands to
meet your needs
to talk or no
join me and give
the gift of you.
You lean into me
give me the strength
To lean back.

TUGGERANONG LAKE

Light racing across
Water rippling under wings
Bird calls to rejoice

FIRE HOUSES

They reckon if you drive into town on a winter's night you can pinpoint all the Blakfullas' homes by the fires in the backyards.

They aren't wrong.

Ice and chill flows over the land with the descent of the sun, till flames bloom in most yards. A small cluster of Blaks huddle around till it's strong enough to chew through blocks of wood. Sourced from the local sawmill that is constantly dying, but never quite dead.

Mum likes all the lights inside off, no TV on either. Nothing but the sounds of wood spitting in flames made crisp with someone grabbing green sticks. Silly one there.

Mismatched chairs pulled close in the circle, stories start. Remember when this happened… or that one there went and… what about the time…

Your face and hands start to burn so you turn like a spit-roasted pig, trying to relieve the intense chill on your back where Jack Frost danced his fingers. Spin, laugh, yarn, turn.

Cousins appear up the darkened driveway, calling out to us. 'Oi, watchu fullas doin?'

Mum always laughs. No one in this house drinks, not normally. But here they come with their flagons or cans. More chairs pulled up, someone's got chips, pass us some cuz. Does that older aunty need a cuppa? Gorn make it there, daughter, niece, bub. Someone female and younger.

A quick dash inside, one turns to ten cups. Another person to carry quick.

More stories then. Laughter. So much laughter. It floats into the air, lifted on the fired heat rising into the heavens.

Life. Love. Mob.

STRANGE WEATHER WE'RE HAVING

Brown land turned bright green
Rainfalls, temps, not seen before
Lovely. Disturbing.

BRINDABELLAS

Towering beauties
Stand witness to change of life
Lifts hearts, return home

JOYCE GRAHAM

"Don't take the marks on your writing to heart. They are all there just to make it better."

Joyce Graham is a Kamilaroi woman from Moree who found her love of poetry as a mature aged student. She plays with words and has used her poetry as a tool for healing.

As an emerging poet she has discovered a passion for passion and writes romantic, epic love poems. Throughout the years she has performed her poetry at various events such as the Two Fires Festival and NAIDOC* Week celebrations. Her poetry was included in *By Close of Business* published in 2013 and *Too Deadly: Our Voice, Our Way, Our Business* published in 2017.

She is a member of the First Nations Australia Writers Network.

*National Aborigines and Islanders Day Observance Committee

SUNLIGHT REMINDER

Everyday sunlight across the face
A constant reminder seen
Life from the past
Rage delivered by fists
Decisions controlled
Isolated, alone
Final courage
Trauma informed
Years gone by still healing
But everyday sunlight across the face
A question still unanswered
What reminds him?

AUTUMN

Brown dry rustling leaf
Windblown across ground chilled air
Autumn, winter soon

MOON LIGHT

So round and full, just like me
Across the night sky you roam
Ceremonies to start
Waiting who else is to come
Baying to your glory
Rustling, branches pushed apart
Finding our way

Shh! Sister listen old ones talkin'
Still that tongue
Be with the oneness
Nanna's voice sings, clapping sticks set the beat.

This is woman's song and dance
Time now for sista to learn, for I have gone through
Ochre marks my skin, now your turn
Still your tongue sista!

We are now summoned, take my hand
Let me lead as lessons you will learn
Meet the old ones you will
No need to struggle, just still your tongue
No conversation needed

BLUE BOTTLE

Family Trip to the Beach

Smell the salty sea breeze so strong could almost taste it
Memories flooding back
Family visit to the beach
Crawling at the water's edge
Small waves gently lapping in

Hot tense burning forearm
Screaming looking for mum
Running as fast as tears
Presenting forearm string of beaded welts

Quick, where is the lifesaver?
Scanning crowd
Yellow and red hard to see
Eyes darting to and fro

Finally,
Hard rubbing sand
Tears still crashing over cheeks
Tentacles gone
Reminding beaded welts red raw

Ahh!!
memories of the sea
carry with me all these years
yet my love for you hasn't waned
just caution remains

BROTHER

Did dad visit you?
Or uncle or grandfather or grandmother?
Was it Willie that called you?
Was it easy to surrender?

Who came with hand outstretched?
That you took easily
Them Old Ones, who did they send?
How did they convince you?

Hard was your life.
Beatings, mocking and accusations
Phone calls of drunken tears and slurs
Or just simply humbuggin', a debt you promise
Brother was life such a battle
Your desire for love
Your desire for approval

Footprints across my heart
Arms empty
Eyes now filled with water
Rivers flow so freely

Questions I have
Was it promise of peace that convinced you?
Was it joy that swayed you?

Or was it just relief?
Tell me now!

Shattered and broken
My younger brother there was no need
Alone you walked
Left me behind
Too soon
No need

HOMELAND

Ancestral Land of mine
Black soil, blistering sun
White workers styling up in town
While poverty suppressed streets

Sacred water not kissed by sun
Aching for your warmth to soothe a broken heart
Healing that calls everyone
Tourist filled christmas streets

Highway stretched long and straight
Plains here I come
Many hours tired with gobbled bitumen
Crying for the lost one, now worried for my son

Arriving in the night, with my heavy heart
I hear your song calling me
For now, we put your soul to rest
All your life I have known you
Left without a goodbye
First to travel the path alone

Homelands I love
But ask you wait for me
For the journey is unknown
Although I am the Elder
Time for you to lead
Perhaps for one last time to visit my homelands

SAMANTHA FAULKNER

"I enjoy the friendship and laughs when we gather as Us Mob Writing group. We support one another as First Nations writers in the ACT."

Samantha is a Torres Strait Islander and Aboriginal woman, from Badu and Moa Islands in the Torres Strait and the Yadhaigana and Wuthathi peoples of Cape York Peninsula, Queensland. She is the proud author of *Life Blong Ali Drummond: A Life in the Torres Strait* (Aboriginal Studies Press, July 2007) and editor of *Pamle: Torres Strait Islanders in Canberra* (2018).

Her poetry and short stories have been published nationally in *Cordite Poetry Review, Verity La Creative Arts Journal, Canberra Times* and *Rabbit Nonfiction Poetry Journal* as well as internationally in *Ora Nui Special Edition: A Collection of Māori and Aboriginal Literature*, and *Narrative Witness: International Writing Program, University of Iowa.*

In 2022, Samantha was awarded a Residential Fellowship at Varuna – The National Writers' House. She is a member of the Australian Capital Territory Aboriginal and Torres Strait Islander Arts Network, and MARION (formerly Australian Capital Territory Writers Centre), as well as the Australian Society of Authors. Samantha is the Treasurer of the First Nations Australia Writers Network and Us Mob Writing group.

ALWAYS WAS, ALWAYS WILL BE

You tell me it's not mine
That it never was
Never will be mine
What would you know?

You taught me English
To read and write
Uncivilised native that I am
What would I know?

You clothed and sheltered me
Educated me
Permitted me to live on your country
What would we know?

More than two hundred years have gone
Look at how far I've come
My ancestors have lived here
From the beginning of time
They've survived, thrived

Languages, art, culture, knowledge
Our gifts to the nation
If only you'd listen
Always was, always will be!

MASTERCHEF

"Too easy," he said
It's a little bit of this
And a little bit of that
Just watch what I'm doing

He stirred and stopped
Drew the aroma to him
Inhaled the magic deeply
And stirred the pot again

The wooden spoon tapped the rim
Lid went on top
Covered our dinner
The lesson almost complete

"Taste it every now and then
You must let it sit
For the flavours to gather
Then re-heat when ready"

How hard can it be?
I thought to myself
I'm watching him make it
I eat this all the time
But I knew then
That with all his years
His dinner was hard to replicate
With the love that went in that day

TIFFANY

"Trauma, I'll show you what fucking trauma is all about," Tiffany yelled as she banged her fist on the table. She stared defiantly across the table at Gary, a non-Indigenous graduate from her cohort.

"Um, I'm sorry," he stammered. "I didn't mean to offend you." Gary responded, not knowing where to look. Up, down, at Tiffany, at their supervisor or out the window.

Tiffany could not believe her ears. How could Gary be so stupid? How could he say that all Aboriginal people should just get over their trauma and get on with Closing The Gap? Yet at the same time, he was white, privileged and middle class. His family sent him to a private school. God, he probably did not even know any Aboriginal people. Maybe she was the first Aboriginal person he had met. She felt sick.

"Well let's bring this meeting to a close," Harry their supervisor said quickly. "Tiffany, please come to my office now."

Great she thought, here I am just standing up for mob and trying to educate this idiot and now I am the one getting in trouble. Unbelievable!

She grabbed her writing pad and pen and followed Harry into his office. End result he gave her a warning as swearing at colleagues in the workplace would not be tolerated. Harry reminded Tiffany of the Australian Public Service Code of Conduct and Values. As a graduate with the Department, Tiffany had to follow these rules.

God, she thought, that's just great. At least she wasn't sacked. Her parents would be furious. Of course, she was not going to tell them. Sure, they supported her through uni and she was still living at home, but they did not need to know about this little setback on her career journey to be a Senior Executive Service Officer. Not when she was only a few months into the graduate program. Fuck this, I'm going shopping, she thought.

***

The next day her department was hosting a morning tea for NAIDOC Week. It was going to be huge as the Secretary was coming and all staff were encouraged to attend. Tiffany was looking forward to it too as it would kill a couple of hours in the day.

Harry walked up to her desk and asked her to come into his office. Uh, oh, she thought. What am I in trouble for now? I don't think I've done anything wrong recently.

Harry closed the door behind her and asked her to sit down. He basically told her that the invited guest speaker Aunty June could not attend the function. She was sick at home with the flu. At the morning meeting of VIPs, Harry had suggested that Tiffany would be a good replacement. He knew that Tiffany was one of the youngest graduates in the department and that her parents were well known and respected in the community. He thought that she would be a great speaker.

Tiffany sat there dumbfounded. There was silence. She hadn't realised that he had stopped talking and was looking at her for a response. "So, what do you think?" Harry eagerly awaited her response.

"Um, sure yeah I guess, I can do it," she replied. Tiffany got up and walked out of his office. The butterflies in her stomach navigated up her body and became a full-blown migraine.

She grabbed her mobile and took the lift down to escape the building. She needed to think, get some fresh air and call someone to talk this over with. She would call her Mum.

Mum thought it was great that Tiffany was asked to give a speech on the NAIDOC theme. "That's perfect," she said. "You could talk about your Nan and what an impact she has had on you," Mum added.

"Yeah, great idea, Mum," Tiffany thanked her. "I gotta go. I have a speech to write."

Later that morning, Tiffany entered the huge conference room on the ground floor. There were already a lot of people waiting with more arriving by the second.

Tiffany was seated next to the Secretary. She had never met him before. She only knew him from his picture in the weekly e-newsletter.

The MC invited her to the podium and everyone was silent to hear her speech. A calmness came over her as she told her colleagues of her Nan and her experiences. Nan was a member of the Stolen Generation and experienced the loss of her family, language and culture. She did get to reunite with her own mother later in life and re-connect with her family who had been waiting a long time for that day to happen.

Tiffany had heard her Nan and Mum tell the story many times. She spoke of how her Nan encouraged her to go to uni, to get a good education and a job. That's why Tiffany was standing there today. Nan was Tiffany's role model.

She received loud applause from the audience and was congratulated by the MC and Secretary. The rest of the event went by in a blur. She was on a high from the speech. Her colleagues came up to congratulate her. She was delighted and exhausted. Nan would be proud of her.

HELLO

Hello green trees, grass
I have missed you a lot
Softens today's news

SOUNDS OF NATURE

Bird calls far away
Beep, beep the truck moves slowly
Parrot flies over

SAMIA GOUDIE

"Listen to those around you, to the stories that are around you and to the world that surrounds you. Don't wait, don't put things off, write as if your life depends on it!"

Samia was born on Ngunnawal and Ngambri Country where she was removed from her Mum due to the policies of the time and adopted. Her Mother's family was from Githabul/Gidabal Country and the Geinyan clan region of the Queensland/New South Wales Border Ranges. She has never known her father. Samia identifies as Queer and Bundjalung.

Samia is a multimedia artist and a member of Us Mob Writing and First Nations Australia Writers Network. Samia's poetry has been published by the International Writing Program Iowa Press, Wakefield Press, Norton and Norton, Aboriginal Studies Press, Recent Work Press and Rutledge Press. Her work has also been published in journals such as *Mascara Literary Review, Cordite Poetry Review, Southerly* and 3CMedia e-journal.

In 2022, she won the Kerry Reed-Gilbert Poets Award by First Nations Australia Writers Network. Samia was a runner up in the Boundless Indigenous Writers Mentorship by Text Publishing and Writing New South Wales. Through this she was invited to take up a Residential Fellowship at Varuna – The National Writers' House. Samia also undertook a residency though the Australian Capital Territory Creative Recovery and Resilience Program, with the Ainslie and Gorman Arts Centres.

The experiences and mentorships offered through these organisations and individuals has provided invaluable support for Samia to write her first novel.

IN THIS VALLEY

In this valley,

generations of glistening gums reach skyward

Roots reaching deep,

Holding earth

I imagine lying here

Warmed by a fire

Billy tea, some damper

My dog and me

Whip birds call and respond

Flashes of sound,

Hisses and hums

Magpies

Shifting light,

Shadow dust, where dry cracked earth lay broken

Creeks now overflow

Food and medicines everywhere

Purple lily, fringe lily,

Casesia Calliantha, Thysanthotus Tuberous,

Daraban, Munong, Yam Daisies, Microcseris Lanceolata,

Mummadya, Cherry Ballarat, Exocarpos Cupressiformis

Cauliflower bush, Cassina Longifolia

I am searching for words, confused at the order, the correct naming

Elusive, beyond my reach, clumsy in my mouth;

Wrapping myself around the silver flesh of a tree

Eyes closed,

I float for just a moment

Suspended... Kissed by the breeze

Dissolving, becoming, returning

As country sings

Above: For Aunty Kerry Reed-Gilbert, 24 October 1956 to 13 July 2019
Previously published as 'Call me by true names' in *Cordite Poetry Review*, 2022

Opposite: Previously published in *A Handful of Sand: Words to the Frontline*, May 2012 (Southerly 71-2), and a stanza included in *Too Afraid to Cry* by Ali Cobby Eckermann, 2012

I AM HERE

YOU call me the nowhere people, I am, to you the unseen,
    the invisible, half of something,
neither white nor black conceived in a racial war
or was it love?
YOU believe the story, lock, stock and poisoned blankets
You believe the lies, flour, sugar and tea.

You tell me "just get over it"
YOU look at me and do not see, and you shame me
and I shame myself
because I am not nowhere
I am everywhere in my belonging I am still here.

YOU are reminded of this Great War
and the casualties, every time I scream,
every time you disown me, push me away
the bones of my ancestors, lie here,
they will not be forgotten,
I will not forget,
in this earth, beneath our feet
they lie wrapped as lovers around tree roots,
now clay and sand and dirt
mingled in layers of moss
I vow this, I will not feed the racist hand
or keep another down I will rise up, WE will rise up,
I am here.

A HANDFUL OF EARTH

A copper's hand hits my jaw
As he rips my push bike from my hands
My tartan school uniform
Tears
As HE throws me to the ground

The crowd roars megaphone loud

What do we want?
LAND RIGHTS
When do we want it?
NOW

Metal and wood clang
the Tent Embassy is torn away
canvas falls to the ground
As I fall to earth

There's red blood on my hand
And yellow daffodils
Black soil in my mouth

I'm eating earth

What do we want
LAND RIGHTS
When do we want it?
NOW

SMALL THINGS

Kindness

It's the small things that make a difference.

On Sundays, everything is closed, no shops or petrol
stations and everyone stays home.

On Sundays
I walk around the block
Past the houses of everyone I know
there's Max and Jenifer with the turtles and the chickens
then the old couple with the soft blue polished Holden
sitting in the drive

Then there's the Paterson kids on the corner
Who I spent my Saturdays with
We'd go for rides doubling up with no hands,
Weaving fearless in the middle of the road.

2 houses further down is where we'd sit and talk,
picking at grass and dandelions and laughing at each other's jokes

And there's our tree house right next door
high up wedged in thick wide limbs
Where we ate cold spaghetti from a tin
And where I smoked my first cigarette and tried to hold it in

Finally,
I'd cross the road and take a shortcut through the park and then the lane way that was safe even in the dark

Just one time I'd felt unsafe but not for what you think
It was a sad story that I didn't understand
of a man called Jock
Who mumbled when he spoke

I'd seen him one day and he looked so scared, he ran off yelling loudly words I couldn't quite make out

I told my Dad
Shell shock, he said and looked so sad
I didn't really understand it, but I knew it must be bad

Of course, I knew of war
I knew a lot of things by then
Kids always know more than others think they do
That's never changed I think

But now I've lost my story's place, I've circled round as stories do,
The shell shock man had stopped me
that wasn't in the plan
But eventually I'll get there
Just past this broken faded fence
The one that my cousin and his brother had tried to fix but he

broke his hand instead

I remember because I mowed the lawn that Saturday for Mrs
Martin who lived next door
he sat and watched me through the window
from on his bed,

Now,
I've left the lane
I pass my best friend's house,
the one with all the sports cars and the dartboard in the garage
where her brothers played loud music,

and occasionally let us in

It wasn't till
much later that I heard she'd died
Head on in a car crash in one of her brothers' cars,

I found out after dinner on a Friday night
when the phone rang whilst we ate our fish and chips
My mother came back shaken
Wordless

I left to go to bed..........

So finally, now I'm here at the old folk's place
Where people's grammas and grandpas go

I knew I'd get fed chocolates and sometimes-even cake
I loved to go

It wasn't just for food make no mistake
I'd grown to love the stories of their lives
the photos from the past,

It felt right and natural these oldies were my friends
Although they were ancient
And hair gone grey
And often mumbled things

It's their stories that kept me coming back, even if it rained

You see it is the small things that matter,
you remember most
Like sitting in the garden and listening to bird song
the smell of baking bread
the warmth of my best friend
My dog called Scamp, lying on my feet

Generosity is the small things

Like the trees that give us shade and fruit
becoming the fuel of fire
that keeps us warm in winter
when it's the perfect time for soup

It's these simple things, small quiet acts of kindness
Like bread freshly made
          left at my front door
                    Without a note

          So, though the world seems jagged
                    and often very cruel

Kindness,
          Like Light,

          Always finds a way
                    to keep on breaking through

Dedication for the Elders and Old people, whose stories as a child kept me strong.
Inspired by Leonard Cohen's words from 'Anthem', "There is a crack, a crack in everything/
That's how the light gets in".

HEART BEAT

My feet sink
Salt licked
                    Seagulls circle
Looking for chips

Waves break slow

Sand glistening

Broken shells

The beach is long
My body is strong
I walk for a long time

And then I rest.

I sit and bury my feet
Zoe my dog
rests her wet head close to my body

I notice the silence
A whispering wind

Purple dune flowers pushing through
Relentless in survival

I wonder at them

My mind shifts
I notice my breath

My Heart beat

I too have survived.

THE IN BETWEEN

Let me lie here

Sinking deep with earth
    Moss green trees
Silver gums shining

Let me lie here

Floating; held by
    deep blue ocean
Crystal clear beneath

Let me lie here

Arms outstretched
    Cradled
In your arms

Hold me
    As I drift

The veil between the worlds
    Softens
        And Lifts
Let me lie here now
    I am ready

To be a newborn star
　　In a galaxy of love
Then
　　Let me go

ELAINE PATRICIA LOMAS

"Language and culture cannot be separated and are intrinsic and inextricable. You cannot separate them and you cannot see where it begins or where it ends."

I was born in Griffith New South Wales and I am a proud and strong Galari Wiradyuri woman. My Ancestral Lands and Cultural connections are between the Marrambidya (Murrambidgee) Galari (Lachlan River) Wambuul (Macquarie) and Castlereagh Rivers in South Western and Central Western New South Wales. I live in Canberra, Australian Capital Territory.

I am a writer, poet and song writer and an experienced public speaker. I have also translated two English language stories into Wiradyuri language, in collaboration with other people. These include *Where Happiness Hides* – written by Anthony Bertini and Jennifer Goldsmith, Wiradjuri language: *Nginha Yiing Durrulgali* – translated by Elaine Patricia Lomas and Letetia Harris, *Just One Bee* – written by Margrete Lamond and Anthony Bertini, Wiradyuri language: *Ngumbaay Ngarru* – translated into Wiradyuri Language by Elaine Patricia Lomas and Candace Cord.

I am teaching Wiradyuri Language Culture and Heritage at Charles Sturt University in Wagga Wagga and various schools in the Riverina Region of New South Wales. I have a Post Graduate Degree in Public Health from the University of New South Wales (November 2013) and Graduate Certificate in Wiradjuri Language Culture, Heritage and Nation Building from Charles Sturt University, Wagga Wagga Campus, New South Wales (December 2018).

MY LITTLE GIRLS

I love their big brown eyes and their mops of curls
And the way they play with each other.
The sloppy kisses of my little girls,
I should because I'm their mother

I love their possessiveness and their little fights
They vie for my attention
The holding of a grubby little hand
It's a part of a mother's affection,

I love their cute little noses
And their great big smiles
And their eagerness to help me
And I'll dry the tears of my little girls
Until all the seas are empty.

A tribute to my daughters, Catherine Alice-Maree Lomas and Bethany Anne-Sharee Lomas Fairley
Elaine Patricia Lomas © 1984

BAA BAA BUDHANG DYUMBAG BAA BAA BLACK SHEEP

BAA BAA BUDHANG DYUMBAG Baa Baa Black Sheep

YAMANDHU GIDYANG DHURAY Have you any wool

NGAWA GIBIR NGAWA GIBIR Yes sir Yes sir

BULA NGUMBAAY GIDYANG Three bags full

NGUMBAAY GIBIR GU One for the Master

NGUMBAAY YINAA GU One for the Dame

NGUMBAAY BIRRANY DYANG GU NGANHA
One for the little boy who

WINYA NGUBILA lived down the lane

Translation in Wiradjuri language by Elaine Patricia Lomas and Letitia Harris © 2019 (Canberra, Australian Capital Territory)
A New Wiradjuri Dictionary by Dr Stan Grant Snr and Dr John Rudder 2010

HOW SCRUB THE DIRTY TURKEY GOT HIS NAME

There's a story going round
They say that truth is sound
About how Scrub the dirty Turkey got his name

Scrub loved to scratch around
His leafy dusty mound
And let the dusty dirt settle in his wings

He'd peck and dig all day
His wings covered in red clay
So happy that he would cackle and sing

Mr Goosey his dear friend
Said "Scrub this must end"
You have to go and clean up in the dam

Your feathers are all stuck
And you're smelly and so yuck
Its time to join the others for the game

See how your wife n daughter
Love to wallow in the water
And a joyous time they have its quite clear

Can't you see you're missing out
That's what families are about
But Scrub the dirty Turkey didn't hear

All the Males and Hens and chicks
Scratched up leaves and dirt and sticks
But scrub the dirty Turkey didn't give a toss

He watched them scratch around
Building nests in leafy mounds
Because Scrub the dirty Turkey was the boss

And when the day would end
On the dam they'd all descend
To splish and splash their feathers they would preen

They'd call out to Old Scrub
Come on down and have a tub
Get out that dirt and your feathers will be clean

But Old Scrub just didn't care
Stuck his plumage in the air
And as he wandered off his wattle swung to and fro

I just don't know why it is
His wife said to her friends
That my Scrub dislikes the dam water so

He would rather go and scratch
In the scrubby brush and patch
And cover his feathers with dirt to nestle down

This behavior made her sad
All the old male Turkeys mad
That they marched him to the dam in town

Well the whole town had heard the squabble
And saw the wibble and the wobble
As they grappled with old Scrub to throw him in

I'm not DIRTY .. that's absurd
Old Scrub's voice could be heard
As he screamed his innocence above the din

It was a sight they won't forget
To see Scrub soaked and wet
His feathers stuck with dirt and greasy grime

Here's the soap old Goosey yelled
And Scrub's feathers spread and held
Got a good washing for the very first time.

Now with his feathers clean and dried
And his family by his side
Scrub proudly walked through the feathered throng

There a gaggling song did sing
Hail Scrub our new clean king
He vowed he'd be while the days he lived were long

Big Mal the Mallee Mayor
Raised his stick high in the air
His booming voice was heard loud and clear

Friends while I have the floor
And Scrub's not dirty anymore
I declare that this day Scrub Day every year

They cheered Hip Hip Hooray
And danced the night away
With Wally Roo and his big bush band

Scrub and Goosey had sore feet
As they fell into their seat
Their legs too tired they couldn't even stand

Now dear old Scrub tells a story
With all the grace and glory
About how he really got his name
They all think it quite quirky
And his tale of the Dirty Turkey
Is spread far and wide with his fame

WIRADJURI NGIYANG

Song Tune: London's burning

Wiradjuri Ngiyang	Wiradjuri Language
Marambangbilang	It's Wonderful
Nguyaguyamilang	It's Beautiful
Walanbangan	It's Very Strong
Murrayarra	Speak Out Loud
Dhuluyarra	Speak In Truth
Yindyamarra	Respect and Honour
Yindyamarra	Respect and Honour
Dyiramadilinya	Be Proud
Dyiramadilinya	Be Proud

A New Wiradjuri Dictionary by Dr Stan Grant Snr and Dr John Rudder 2010

THE CLOWN

EVERYONE IS SAD IN TOWN,
I KNOW WHAT, THEY NEED A FUNNY CLOWN
HE'LL MAKE THEM LAUGH AND DANCE AND SING
WHAT HAPPINESS THAT WOULD BRING
FOR EVERYONE FROM MILES AROUND
MAYBE EVERY TOWN SHOULD HAVE A CLOWN

BALADHU WIRADYURI

Song Tune: Frère Jacques

Baladhu Wiradyuri	I am Wiradyuri
Baladhu Wiradyuri	I am Wiradyuri
Ngawa Baladhu	yes I am
Ngawa Baladhu	yes I am
Dyirimadilinya bu	I am proud and
Walangang Baladhu	very strong I am
Ngawa Walangang	yes very strong
Ngawa Walangang	yes very strong
Ngawa Baladhu	yes I am
Ngawa Baladhu	yes I am

A New Wiradjuri Dictionary by Dr Stan Grant Snr and Dr John Rudder 2010

MY TIN HUMPY HOME

My mind goes back to my Tin Humpy Home,
where my spirit ran freely and the channel swiftly flows,
with its hardened earthen floors and the big open fire,
where a camp oven swings on a hook of strong wire.

The smell of Johnny cakes called us quickly to rise,
we would rush from our bed wiping sleep from our eyes,
topped with leftover rabbit or curried Emu eggs,
all good food to fill our strong hollow legs.

There was sweet smells of wild wattle and rows of geraniums,
wild daisies and marigolds and the grape seeded chook runs.
The garden with outlines of green and brown bottles,
all neatly weeded with no cat's eyes or nettles.

At Christmas we'd decorate the small Cyprus trees,
with coloured crepe paper, yellow, red, blue and green,
we take bottle tops and tie them with string,
bits of broken glass and tin lids were our baubles and bling.

There the trains rolled by and the mulga bush grew we played our
games without toys or shoes.
At night we'd fall asleep with the rain on the roof while our Elders
told stories and sang the songs of their youth.
We'd fall asleep to the pots catching the drips, and dream about
our next family trips.

Our Koori churches made of bough sheds or wood with no steeple, where our cousins, Aunties and Uncles sang the Hymns of our Old people.
The Old Rugged Cross sang with harmonies abound, and God told his Angels he too wanted that sound.

Our family trapped rabbits and picked vegies and fruit.
Life for us kids was nothing more than a hoot.
We lived hand to mouth day to day,
with so many cousins and games to play,
like hidey go seek and come over red rover,
or we'd swim in the channel after rolling in clover.

Material things we didn't have very much,
but our tin humpy home had that family touch,
no screen doors or glassed in windows,
there were cut out tin holes where the fresh air flows.

We sat on rugged stools or kerosene drums,
they were so hard made your buble so numb,
but after fifty years of leaving these memories are still clear, like last night's rain it fills my eyes with tears.
If that ground could talk or the trees broke into song,
I know they would say come back home, where you belong.

Elaine Patricia Lomas © 2012 (Mt Druitt, New South Wales)

GREAT LAND WIRADYURI

Song Tune: Galway Bay

If you ever come across the seas to Oz land
Well maybe at the closing of the day
You can sit and watch the moon rise over Wagga
And see the sun go down somewhere near Hay.

Just to hear again the ripple of the Bidya
See the women catching fish along it's banks
To eat beside the campfire near a humpy
And hear our dear old father giving thanks.

The strangers came they tried to teach us their ways
They scorned us for being what we are
Well they might as well go chasing after rainbows
Or light a night time fire from a star.

Now if there's gonna be a life hereafter
And somehow I am sure it's gonna be
I will ask my God to let me make my Heaven
In that great land that is Wiradjuri,
Oh in that great land that is Wiradjuri.

Words rewritten by Dr Stan Grant Snr and Elaine Patricia Lomas © 2010

ODETTE FULLER

"Being able to read so many First Nations books has been like seeing our own voices, stories that are relevant to us, our truths. It's inspirational."

Odette Fuller is a Wuilli Wuilli woman from Eidsvold, Queensland, and descendant from the Gooreng Gooreng and Wakka Wakka peoples. Odette was born in Eidsvold, but moved around a lot, which she was thankful for as she met so many different First Nations people, heard their stories and realised that a lot of those stories were very similar to hers.

Odette is a mother of two, grandmother of seven, as well as helping bring up some of her nieces, nephews and other extended families throughout the years. She has worked for a number of Aboriginal organisations, and has continued to update her skills through education, as she believes it is the key.

She currently lives and works in Canberra but makes trips home regularly to connect to her Country.

PORCUPINE

Waddling through the bush
Big juicy fat fella
Feed a mob tonight

BURNETT SALMON

Night on the river
The eerie sighs and gasps
Old Ceratodus

UNDERCOVER BROTHER

Johnny (the little stonehead) had to move in with me cause the dickhead was spending all his money on the TAB and yarndhi. You wouldn't believe he was older than me by three years. When he was stoned, he was the most annoying fucking person to be around. He knew my side was really sensitive so he'd come up looking for laughs and keep poking me and making me jump. I'd be screaming at him to stop, but the idiot just didn't get it into his fogged up head.

He'd get my four-year-old daughter, and they'd start telling each other knock knock jokes. Shit didn't even make sense but it made that moron laugh.

He'd bring these red split ice-creams home for my niece and nephew, who were both badly hyperactive. We figured out that dickhead knew that the additives were making them go worse than usual. He would sit there in stitches laughing as they full on zoomed around the house.

He had a couple of yarndhi plants growing along the river and he'd go out every now and then to pick some leaves off, and dry them under my grill, I don't know how many times I went off at him for doing that cause the smell would go through my flat. One night he came home and I was busy getting the kids bathed and into bed. Once I got them settled, I walked into the kitchen, he's sitting there eating a big plate of steak and eggs. It looked lovely, he looked up and seen me watching him and reckon. "Sis, don't ask me for any, I got the munchies really bad." I was trying to talk him into giving me some and that selfish bastard started spitting all over his food so he wouldn't have to share. Spiteful bitch.

He started getting these Rastafarian magazines on how to grow yarndhi and start dreadlocks. One morning, before he started living with me, he came and asked if I had any old contraceptive pills laying around. I asked him what he wanted those for. He reckons he read somewhere that they make a really good fertilizer crushed up with chicken shit for growing good yarndhi. Just shook my head and gave him the bloody pills.

Then he came up with this scheme that rubbing conditioner all through this hair would begin the dreadlock process. He did it, it didn't work. What a dumb arse.

He eventually got dreadlocks, they were down to his arse, but he shit himself when he read this article about a man who had redbacks in his dreads, so he cut them off years later.

His hair was still long but he had a massive, big grey beard by then and long hair. We were walking down the street one cattle sale day, so everyone was in town, white and black. His mate Rossy drove past us and screamed out, "Osama Bin Laden, ya cunt". Shame job, everyone was looking at us. When I looked at photos of my brother, he kinda did look like Bin Laden, WTF.

Another time, he went and bought himself this second-hand golden panel van. Don't ask me how he never got pulled up in it, cause I can't remember ever seeing him driving straight in it, he was always off his head. I never hopped in the car with him unless I was desperate. One night he came home for a feed. I'd never seen him so stoned before, his eyes were just slits and he could barely talk. He had a feed and yelled out he was going. Next thing I heard this almighty crash. I run out, the car was smashed into this big pole, he was bent over the steering wheel. I'm running and screaming towards the car. I was shaking, I thought he was really hurt. When I got to the window, I realized he was bent over the steering wheel laughing. I started cracking up at him, he just put the car in reverse and drove off down the road laughing.

"This bastard is going to give me a heart attack."

CALLING OF THE LAND

Not feeling too good
My land calling me
Go home to recharge

ELDERS ADVICE

Another crazy night at the Star Hotel. Walking into the black fellas side for Sunday session, 'Brown Eyed Girl' blasts from the jukebox, my two deaf-as-post uncles standing in the front doorway whispering together (beats the shit out of me how they hear each other). I see my brother at his table with all his yarndhi gang, eyes slitted, too stoned to say much with stupid grins on their faces. At another table is my three cousins, one with his woman sitting there head down. Seen that bullshit before. She's not allowed to look anywhere because she could be eyeing off another man. Pfft. He's the one who is the biggest man-whore going. My Aunty Fay is sitting with all her younger nieces and nephews. She always hangs around us young ones, we love her. She tells the dirtiest jokes and says the most random shit, its hysterical. She once made up a song when we all partying called 'Nookie in the grandstand'.

I grab a shandy and go to walk out to Aunty Fay's table when my cousin Lori stops me.

'Sis, you seen Jace around?

I tell her no, I'm not keeping tabs on her slut of a man. I wish she'd just dump his ass.

He's been rooting around with this other one named Trish. The whole freakin town knows about it, so it isn't as if Lori didn't know. You can't fart in this town without everyone smelling it. She heads off to the white fellas side to find him.

Sitting at the table with Aunty Fay and my family there's a loud screaming, a lot of swearing. Looking outside, we can see Lori and Trish going for it, punch for punch, and pulling each other's hair. My cousin Jack got up to ref the fight to make sure it was fair – no kicking, double banking, just fists.

It goes on for about ten minutes before Jack calls it off cause Trish is bleeding from the nose. Lori comes crying over to our table, hair everywhere, a few scratches on her face and neck and a bit of a busted lip. Someone passed her a beer. Once she calms down a bit Aunty Fay looks at her patting her back and says real sympathetic, 'Look bub, don't worry about him, when budoo not pointin in your direction, go find another one. Plenty of budoo out there.'

The table goes real quiet. Then everyone just collapses in laughter, even Lori the dickhead, is laughing and trying not to split her lip any further. Told you, this place is womba town.

LEARNING HOW TO COOK

Looking after my two teenage sisters after Mum passed away, and Dad turned to grog, cause he couldn't handle it without her, was hard. Especially being a single parent to two young children of my own. I couldn't stop them drinking on the weekends, but my rule was if they stayed with me they had to complete grade ten. We had so many fights over it, but they stuck to it most of the time. My second youngest sister, Debra, had the most beautiful black skin, tall and deadly figure. She was attached to the hip with our cousin Lorna. Those two got up to more than I'd like to know about. My baby sister Lindy Lou, who was a lot fairer (took after my grandmother's side), used to get around with another cousin her age, Aggie. They made ya weak. They watched Grease about 100 times and formed their own Pink Ladies (blackest pink ladies I ever saw). They had one leather jacket between them. Someone wrote pink ladies on it for them and they used to take turns wearing it. I heard so many fights over that fucking pink jacket. We even had our own urban cowboys, after that movie came out and all our young fellas loved it.

One of the things that really pissed me off was that they were so dependent on me for food, so I decided I was going to teach them how to cook. One night I had stewing steak out.

I told Linda and Agnes they had to cook it, gave them the instructions, and left them to it. After a fair while they told me it was ready, when I looked in the pot, it was basically bits of meat and vegetables floating around in that much water, there was barely any taste. My big daughter reckons, "I'm not eating that". Linda and Agnes got really pissed off and stalked away muttering shit about starving then.

A couple of nights later I asked Debra and Lorna to cook up meat and gravy. I explained everything to them and asked if they were alright to go ahead with it. They both nodded yes, so I left them to it. Half an hour later I heard my brother Johnny coming home, which probably meant he had the munchies and was looking for something to eat (that dickhead thought my flat was a fucking restaurant). Next thing I heard him going off, he started yelling out to me to come fix the gravy up cause he was starving. When I walked into the kitchen and looked at the pan, the wooden spoon was standing straight up in this white "gravy". I'm pissing myself laughing, Johnny's begging me to fix it up. "I can't eat that shit, it'll clog me up for a week. Come on sis, fix it."

I told him not to be stupid you can't fix that; it's too far gone. Dickhead had to go find food somewhere else.

By this time Debra and Lorna had gotten the shits badly, swearing and carrying on, they both took off into the room and wouldn't talk to us. Both my sisters are a lot older now, and are amazing cooks, lol.

AFTER THE FLOODS

All along the river
Bodies of old ghost gums
Dying on the bank

JESSIKA SPENCER

"Being a part of a First Nations' writers group is powerful."

Jessika is a Wiradjuri woman from the Sandhills of Narrungdera, New South Wales. For over the past decade she has resided on beautiful Ngunnawal/Ngambri Country, where she currently creates her art.

Through her varied art forms, Jessika explores her cultural identity. She does this via photography, poetry, writing, activism and both contemporary and traditional weaving.

Being a First Nations woman, culture and literature go hand in hand. They are intertwined and are an ongoing source of inspiration for her.

Within the writing arena, Jessika's goals and ambitions are to write novels, produce poetry books and create meaningful children's literature.

She was guided and welcomed into Us Mob Writing by Aunty Kerry Reed-Gilbert and this connection has helped her grow immensely.

LET HIM GO

It's like trying to trap a
butterfly
in a cage,
it's cruel to limit you
for my own
obsessive ways

Let him go

BLOOM

I have spent my entire life
waiting for this moment
holding back
self-contained

But now I am
ready
in full force,
there is nothing I lack
pull the curtains back
   let's begin

BLOODLINES

"If we have children, will they be Aboriginal?"
my Irish ex-boyfriend
asks me seriously,
scrutinising my facial expression

The ignorance stuns me
what else could an
Aboriginal woman produce
if not Aboriginal children?

"What percentage are you?"
a white woman asks me
waiting for me to
answer back with a statistic

I am silent
all the while thinking
of my Nan's stories
from back home on the mission,
of dancing on the sandhills

"But you don't look Aboriginal"
I am told in the
middle of a meeting
in my first month of working
as an "Indigenous Trainee"

My heart sinks and anger flares
as though my fair skin
isn't the result of genocide,
assimilation,
and the white policy;

As though my skin tone
isn't the result
of what your ancestors
did to mine

I am my country
just as my country,
culture and community
are me
those songlines,
bloodlines
run deep

WESTERN BEAUTY STANDARDS

I pluck
and brush
and comb
and bleed
and I still do not
measure up
to their unreachable
ideals of beauty

I wax
and file
and shave
and knead
out all of my larger
bits to
make them more
digestible,
more presentable

And yet I still
cannot reach
those standards
that I fall short of,
they are an
unsurmountable hill

CHOKE

I am the cliff face
of the mountains,
the uneven escarpment
that scales my
insides,

A clean
steep
drop down
into the deep
sea below,

I am no longer
filing,
smoothing,
or removing
my awaiting
jagged edges
for anyone

MARISSA MCDOWELL

"As a member of Us Mob Writing, having our voices and lived experience come to life through our written work gives others a window into our unique perspectives and culture as Australian First Nations' peoples."

Marissa McDowell is a Wiradyuri woman from Cowra, New South Wales. She is the Head of Commissions for the National Indigenous Television, News and Programs/Special Broadcasting Service. Marissa was previously the creative producer for Black & White Films and has worked with Indigenous communities telling their stories through multimedia platforms across Australia.

She is a member of the First Nations Australia Writers Network and Chairperson for Us Mob Writing. Her poetry has been published in the literary journal *Ora Nui Special Edition: a collection of Māori and Aboriginal Literature* (2013) and Overland's *Emerging Poet Series*. She was featured as a contributor in *A Pocketful of Leadership, Too Deadly: Our Voice, Our Way, Our Business, Haiku 4 You Poetic City, Kamberra Many Nations, One Country, Rabbit Nonfiction Poetry Journal 33 ASIA 2021* and *Rabbit Nonfiction Poetry Journal 36 ART 2022*.

Her exhibitions include the Sydney Living Museum, PhotoAccess, Belconnen Arts Centre and Tuggeranong Arts Centre. She has received her Master of Arts Screen Business and Leadership at the Australian Film Television and Radio School, Bachelor of Arts Honours and Bachelor of Media Arts from the University of Canberra, Graduate Certificate in Wiradjuri Language, Culture and Heritage from Charles Sturt University and an Advanced Diploma in Media Arts and Production from the Canberra Institute of Technology.

CAMP DOG

Wiry hair, tawny brown, black stripes
brindle covered her frail body
long sweeping eyelashes framed her sad brown eyes
weathered face
smiling at people while walking by
tail wagging furiously from side to side
looking for attention, a smile, a pat, maybe a treat
scrawny bones, rib cage full, belly protruding
padding on feet cracked flat and bleeding
stumpy but strong legs
carried the weight of her tiny frame
life growing inside her
a litter, her five babies
malnourished, abandoned
a mongrel mix breed of other mixed breeds
lonely, scared, unloved and hungry
camp dog
got no name
everyone's responsibility but no one's to own

A tribute to Liana J Fowler

URBAN

Hustle of the city
Traffic, coffee, graffiti art,
Concrete jungle pace

REBIRTH

Green shoots, trees, grass, hills
Birds singing, flying, blue skies
Fresh air, alive, breathing, safe

THE BROWNING

Long lines waiting outside the supermarket door
check out chick counting 55, 56, 57, 58, you can go in now
stay 1.5 metres away from the person in front
stand on your dot marked clearly on the floor
pray the person behind you doesn't get any closer
breathing down your neck
hairs standing to attention
the person behind you is breaking the 1.5 metre rule
eyes bulging, fixed forward
lip curling, face turning red
yeast, flour, cake mix
everyone's baking bread, cakes, scones, biscuits
none left on the shelves
pasta, rice, and bread
one slightly demented loaf of bread in the bakery section
everyone loading up on carbs
putting on COVID kilos during lockdown
soap, hand sanitiser
everyone sterile
hands dry, cracked and bleeding but clean
everyone washing
the line is moving closer to the register
stay 1.5 metres away from the person in front
someone sneezes
everyone turns, glares
oh my God they must have it!

close your mouth, look forward
don't touch anything, clasp hands together tightly
toilet paper
gone, nothing left
trolleys loaded to the top with rolls of toilet paper
self-service, finally
ushered to every second checkout with plastic protection walls
home finally
quick, run for the toilet
last roll of toilet paper
finger breaks through the paper
revealing the browning
no soap, no steriliser, no toilet paper
COVID.

SPARKLY ONE

Mr Dinosaur orange skin striped belly white, green and purple
cheaply made fibres stuffed with soft down
prize-winning gift from a local side show alley or show game
can't remember
gifted by Aunty
loved so dearly
tucked into bed at night
you are safe
favourite faded blue dress with printed green whales
wrapped around your three-year-old tiny body
toilet training
little accidents
you did it!
joy shared with Mr Dinosaur
headfirst facing straight down into the toilet bowl
first glance of success
you proclaim 'look at the sparkly one' with joy

A tribute to Kaitlyn G Fowler

DATE NIGHT

Clickity clack
my sparkling red shoes shine brightly
under the pale moon light
I click my heels one more time for good luck
clickity clack
red ruby lipstick accentuates my thin lips
maybe I'll get lucky tonight
hair crimped, tied into a high half ponytail
short denim skirt barely covers my lace knickers
ladders in my black tights reveal my freshly shaved,
silky smooth legs
drenched in cheap perfume
cars drive up and down the usually quiet street
engines revving louder faster louder faster
I see him glance at me
bright colours line the sidewalk
girls dressed to impress
eyelashes beckoning the one they are directed at to come
he moves closer
I click my heels one more time
clickity clack
the engines rev louder, faster, louder, faster, louder, faster
my heart is beating, pounding
I lean towards him as he approaches
he smiles, I take a step closer

he takes a step, and kisses the girl dressed to impress beside me
under the pale moon light.

PEACHES AND CREAM

Terry towelling shorts, white t-shirt with blue trim,
embellished printed monkey.
Monkey, the nickname I was given by my two sisters
long lanky limbs, brown skin, dark hair and eyes.

Hanging upside down in the backyard on our old secondhand swing set.
Weathered, thick layers of chipped paint reveal many years of love.

The smell of freshly cut grass, four leaf clovers, dandelions, bindis, scorching summer sun.
Sprinkler spinning, wetting the ground leaving tiny pockets of puddles.
Cooling off dipped toes in little puddles while standing under the sprinkler.

Old yellow barbie bus travelling across the bumpy lawn
barbie driving with her companions onboard a backyard adventure.

Devon sandwiches smeared with tomato sauce on white bread
Cottee's Lime Cordial in plastic cups
frozen oranges in an empty ice-cream container.
Rainbow Brite calls out to Peaches and Cream 'come to my party,
Care Bears, Strawberry Shortcake and Ken are invited too'!

They arrive in style on a yellow Banana Board with red flashy wheels.
Underneath the trampoline is a palace fit for She-Ra, Princess of Power.
The party is pumping, Golden Dream is the life of the party until Pretty in Pink arrives.

The Walkman is playing a mixtape of Bananarama, Joan Jett and Foreigner.

Dogs barking, I'm bored!

I jump onto my trusty rusty old blue
sisters weaving down the streets on their gallant metal rides
friends on bikes join our convoy.

Local corner shop 20c bags of delicious sugary sweetness
Musk Sticks, Fags, Lifesavers, Wizz Fizz
Double Dip, Choo Choo Bars
Red and Green Frogs

THE BEST!

Frozen Sunny Boys
Raspberry
Cola and
Lime

Ride the hilly back streets across the town
streetlight's flicker signalling us
home again.

Let's do it all again tomorrow
the 1980's.

Growing up on Wiradyuri Country (1980's Cowra, New South Wales)

RUSSELL

Chubby little thighs
tight dark curls frame your baby face
chocolate coloured freckles, kissed by the sun
rosy, red cheeks and pouty lips
can barely string a couple of sentences together
high pitch squeals along with looks of uncertainty
for this strange thing you've never seen before
relief washes over you once you see it is harmless
the arrival of a new puppy
big sisters call him Russell
A fitting human name for a kelpie cross poodle
chocolate brown with tight curls just like you
you can't contain the excitement
bubbling inside of your nearly two-year-old tiny body
diving headfirst into Russell's bed
rolling on top of him, squashing him
you play with this new bundle of moving fur with four legs
you flip from side to side around his bed
big enough to fit you both in
your sisters watch on as you become acquainted
you squeal with delight exploding with happiness
'Oh, Russell boy' you say in the sweetest little voice
as you continue to roll on top of him
your four-legged fur friend
Russell.

A tribute to Elyse Fowler

BARRINA SOUTH

"Creativity is the difference between a leader and a follower."

Barrina is a Barkindji woman who is an artist, critic and poet dedicated to writing about topics and themes affecting land, place, culture, and history.

Recently, Barrina was one of five Australian poets selected to participate in the 'Invisible Walls: Poetry as a Doorway to Intercultural Understanding' project paired with a Korean poet to explore cross-cultural dialogue. This project is an initiative run in partnership with the University of South Australia and Sogang University, Seoul, South Korea. In the same year, Barrina was Writer in Residence at the University of Canberra, her poetry was published in *The Art Issue, 36, Rabbit Nonfiction Poetry Journal* and the special issue of the *Teesta Review: A Journal of Poetry*, Kolkata, India.

As an Indigenous academic, Barrina has demonstrated as part of a Bachelor of Arts Degree with Honours the important role New South Wales Tiddas' autobiographical narrative plays in educating the wider audience of Aboriginal women's lived experiences. Barrina is a current member of the First Nations Australia Writers Network, a Director of Us Mob Writing and a contributor and editor of *Too Deadly: Our Voice, Our Way, Our Business*.

UNTITLED

I remember the day the sky died
arms hung heavy from my shoulders
feet were slow to move
head too heavy to lift

I would reach the edge, it was going to take time
focussed on the horizon
aim was to keep moving
temptation was to lie down

I conjured up the courage, forced myself to fall
faced down, grit coated my lips
dust filled my nostrils
waiting, hoping someone might discover me before dark

CLOTH

A piece of torn cloth has caught my eye
        hooked on the barb wire
trying to be free, flapping in Morse, help me
                It gives up its fight
        when the wind leaves it alone
faded, a captive for some time
                A loose thread flies on its own
                        a sign of hope for the others

BRENDA GIFFORD

"Writing gives you opportunity to express your culture with words"

Brenda is a proud First Nations, Yuin woman born in Nowra New South Wales from the Wreck Bay area. Her Country, community and culture are the basis of her arts practice. She is a contemporary classical composer and creates music for ensembles, orchestras, choirs, dance and theatre performances, festivals and concerts. She works collaboratively and is a classically trained saxophonist and pianist. Her music has been performed at venues such as the Sydney Opera House and internationally, and is available through ABC Classical Music.

Brenda is currently a composer, music writer and works in the Arts sector. She joined Us Mob Writing group in 2017 when Aunty Kerry Reed-Gilbert encouraged her to develop her creative side. Her writing style is a mixture of music, short stories and poetry. She is inspired by Aunty Kerry Reed-Gilbert with her writing, as well as Kevin Gilbert. Additionally, she is inspired by artists such as Bart Willoughby, Kev Carmody and Billie Holiday. Her goal is to write music and a novel about Aboriginal music. Brenda's writing has featured in *Too Deadly: Our Voice, Our Way, Our Business* in 2017. In 2019 she was awarded a Bundanoon Trust First Peoples Residency, New South Wales.

www.brendagiffordmusic.com

COUNTRY

I am Yuin
Country is music to me
Play on

A long journey
My spirit now free
Enveloped by mother earth

Saltwater cleanses
Floating
Yuin and Budawang called

Time immemorial
Country

MIRIWA

I am the Miriwa Milumba
I am the Mungalo binda bindaaa

I am the sky shining
I am the clouds rising
Miriwa Miriwa

I am the Miriwa Milumba
I am the Mungalo binda, bindaaa
Miriwa

I wrote this piece as part of the Ngara Burria First Nations Composition course in 2019. I wrote the first verse in Dhurgha language to give voice to our language, then the second verse in English, then the third verse in Dhurga language. It was important for the opening section of the song to be in language. To pay respect to our culture. This project gave me an opportunity to write something that gave voice to our language, for it to be heard and recorded by Ensemble Offspring was great. I wrote this to celebrate the sky and its infinite beauty.

YANGGA

Yangga
Yangga Yangga
Sing

Wuda country
Wuda wuda country
Beautiful country
Wuda minga began
Wuda wuda minga began

Ngara
Ngara ngara our voices

Sing for life Sing for ancestors
Sing for life Sing for ancestors
Ancestors

Ngara our voices
Ngara Ngara our voices

Yangga
sing
Yangga Yangga

Written in the Dhurga language of my people

ABOUT US MOB WRITING

Us Mob Writing group is made up of Aboriginal and Torres Strait Islander poets, writers and storytellers based in Canberra and the surrounding areas. Our members past and present have written poetry, plays, songs, documentary films, short films, television dramas, children's story books, novels, short stories, biographies and autobiographies.

Us Mob Writing group members have included major national and international literary award winners, a national literary awards judge, and multiple nationally and internationally published, performed and produced writers, including winners of the David Unaipon Award.

Members' poetry and prose have been published in many journals and anthologies nationally and internationally, including in the *Macquarie PEN Anthology of Australian Literature*. Their work has been translated to French, Korean, Bengali, Dutch and other languages.

Us Mob Writing have previously published *By Close of Business,* a poetry anthology in 2013 and *Too Deadly: Our Voice, Our Way, Our Business* in 2017. Us Mob Writing members continually promote and showcase First Nations Australian poetry nationally and internationally.

BELINDA NELSON-MCDOWELL

Belinda is a Wiradjuri artist from Cowra, New South Wales. Her artwork has been commissioned and featured in a number of Government organisations, advertisements and is privately collected.

The cover artwork commissioned for *Kuracca*, 'Yinaagalang-dhu yarra giilang-galang ngurambang-ga', is about many Indigenous women gathering together and telling story on Country. These women are from the bush, desert, saltwater and freshwater Country from across the nation.

The Wiradjuri translation is by Elaine Patricia Lomas and Letetia Harris. The Wiradjuri words were taken from *A New Wiradjuri Dictionary* compiled by Dr Stan Grant Snr and Dr John Rudder, 2010.

The cover artwork commission was made possible through the assistance of the Aboriginal and Torres Strait Islander Leadership Grant supported by the Australian Capital Territory Government.